DANGEROUS DRUGS

LSD AND OTHER HALLUCINOGENS

CHRISTINE PETERSEN

W Cavendish
Square
New York

PUBLISHED IN 2014 BY CAVENDISH SQUARE PUBLISHING, LLC
303 PARK AVENUE SOUTH, SUITE 1247, NEW YORK, NY 10010

LIBRARY OF CONGRESS CATALOGING-IN-PUBLICATION DATA
Petersen, Christine.
LSD and other hallucinogens / by Christine Petersen.
p. cm. — (Dangerous drugs)
Includes index.
ISBN 978-1-62712-384-6 (hardcover) ISBN 978-1-62712-385-3 (paperback)
ISBN 978-1-62712-386-0 (ebook)
1. LSD (Drug) — Juvenile literature. 2. Hallucinogenic drugs — Juvenile literature. I. Petersen, Christine.
II. Title.
RM666.L88 P48 2014
615.7883—dc23

EDITORIAL DIRECTOR: Dean Miller
SENIOR EDITOR: Peter Mavrikis
SERIES DESIGNER: Kristen Branch

Photo research by Kristen Branch

The photographs in this book are used by permission and through the courtesy of: Cover photo by David Hoffman Photo Library/Alamy; David Hoffman Photo Library/Alamy, 1; Brandtner & Staedeli/SuperStock, 4; David Q. Cavagnaro/Photolibrary/Getty Images, 7; Psychonaught/Pink Elephants on Parade Blotter LSD Dumbo/Own work, 9; © Gennady Kravetsky/KALIUM/age fotostock, 9; © Johan De Meester/PHILIPPE CLEMENT/age fotostock, 13; © ImageSource/age fotostock, 13; © Brian Durell/age fotostock, 13; ALFREDO ESTRELLA/AFP/Getty Images, 17; AntiMartina/E+/Getty Images, 17; akg-images/Niklaus Stauss/Newscom, 18; image by Jack Vimes/Flickr/Getty Images, 20; Andrew Whittuck/Redferns/Getty Images, 22; Dario Mitidieri/Photonica World/Getty Images, 24; Diverse Images/UIG/Universal Images Group/Getty Images, 26; Diverse Images/UIG/Universal Images Group/Getty Images, 26; © Darrin Jenkins/Alamy, 26; Exactostock/SuperStock, 29; © leonello calvetti/Shutterstock.com, 31; © BURGER/PHANIE/SARL PHANIE/age fotostock, 36; © Laurence Mouton/age fotostock, 37; Biosphoto/SuperStock, 39; AP Photo/RCMP, The Canadian Press, 41; © Robert Matton AB/Alamy, 43; clearstockconcepts/E+/Getty Images, 45; © paul prescott/Alamy, 47; © Hero/Fancy/age fotostock, 50; Tucker Ransom/Archive Photos/Getty Images, 51; © MENDIL/BSIP/age fotostock, 53.

Printed in the United States of America

CONTENTS

CHAPTER ONE

Haunting Hallucinogens

ON A LATE SUMMER DAY IN 1951, DOCTORS in the French town of Pont-Saint-Esprit began to hear reports of food poisoning. Dozens of people complained of chills, nausea, and terrible stomach pains. They fell into bed, unable to walk as their muscles trembled and shook.

While most of the patients began to recover after a few days, others suddenly became much more ill. The victims writhed in misery, crying out that bugs were crawling on their skin. Unable to sleep, they stared into space and mumbled to themselves. Many fearfully described seeing gruesome or scary creatures around them. One man believed he was an

Left: When hallucinating, a person may see or hear things that do not really exist.

airplane. He died after leaping from his upper-story apartment. An elderly woman saw flames all over her body and jumped through her window while trying to put them out.

Investigators learned that all of the patients had eaten bread from the same bakery. They had apparently been poisoned by something in the bread. There was nothing that could be done to help them. People simply suffered until their bodies cleared out the toxin. For some, this took weeks. Others never completely recovered.

Many experts believe the people of Pont-Saint-Esprit ate bread infected by ergot. This organism infests grain crops such as rye. It is a fungus, like mushrooms, though it looks quite different. Ergot is easily mistaken for a large, dark clump of rye seeds. People sometimes harvested the grain without realizing it was infected. At those times, ergot was baked into rye bread and other foods and eaten by the whole community. Thousands of people died from ergot poisoning, especially in Europe during the Middle Ages (400–1600 CE).

It's All in the Alkaloids

How does ergot cause such terrible symptoms? Like many fungi and plants, it produces powerful **alkaloids**.

6

In centuries past, the ergot fungus often grew among grain crops and sickened people who ate the infested grain.

These chemicals evolved as a defense against herbivores (plant-eating animals). Some alkaloids are extremely bitter. Animals hate the taste and may vomit after eating. It's a lesson learned the hard way. The animal will never eat that specific plant again. Other alkaloid chemicals are toxic enough to kill. Atropine is a good example. This alkaloid is found in some nightshade plants.

Alkaloids cause a variety of symptoms in humans. Our reactions depend on the amount consumed. For example, tiny **doses** of ergot increase heart rate and blood pressure. The person may feel energized and joyful. At slightly higher concentrations, the user begins to feel weak and shaky. The skin tingles or goes numb. Nausea, dizziness, and sweating are common. Ergot can also produce **hallucinations** like those experienced by people in Pont-Saint-Esprit. When hallucinating, a person sees, hears, and feels things that are not really there.

Other fungi and plants contain alkaloids that can produce hallucinations in humans. These include psilocybin mushrooms and fly agaric mushrooms, peyote cactus, and plants in the nightshade family. Despite the risks, all of these have been used as **drugs**. A drug is any substance that changes how the brain or body functions. Drugs are classified into groups based on their effects. "Magic" mushrooms, peyote, and nightshade plants are all **hallucinogens**. Ergot is not taken as a drug, but chemicals collected from the fungus are used to **synthesize** lysergic acid diethylamide (LSD) in laboratories. This is the most powerful hallucinogen ever discovered.

Three Types of Hallucinogens

Whether natural or synthetic, hallucinogenic drugs have one thing in common: they change users' thinking, mood,

8

and perception of reality through the senses. Other effects are used to divide the group into smaller categories. These include psychedelic, dissociative, and deliriant drugs. **Psychedelic** drugs make objects look strange, with brilliant colors or melting edges. The person may feel as if they are living in a dream. Emotions can swing wildly, from joy to deep sorrow in seconds.

LSD is considered the "typical" psychedelic. You might recognize this drug by its street names that include acid and blotter. It is the most powerful mind-altering drug ever discovered. Just 30 micrograms of LSD produces intense changes in the human brain. That tiny dose can affect a person for up to twelve hours. How small is that dose? For comparison, a piece of your hair measuring 0.16 inches (4 millimeters) also weighs about 30 micrograms.

Crystalline LSD is often mixed with alcohol and soaked into other materials to produce doses in a variety of forms."

9

LSD is a synthetic hallucinogen but it is made from ergot alkaloids. The fine, white crystals are consumed in several ways. They may be dissolved in alcohol. Absorbent paper is then soaked in the mixture. These sheets may be imprinted with rows of tiny cartoon characters, product logos, or other colorful designs to make them seem appealing. When the paper dries, it is cut into tiny squares. Each holds one design, indicating it is one dose. LSD can also be mixed with gelatin and molded in thin sheets. This "windowpane acid" is also cut into squares and swallowed. LSD is even poured onto sugar cubes. It is sometimes sold as tablets or capsules.

Psilocybin and fly agaric mushrooms are natural psychedelics. These are sometimes called "magic" mushrooms because of their effects. Of approximately 14,000 mushroom species known in the world, 80 percent are toxic to humans. Poisonous and edible species often look alike, and mistakes can be deadly. Peyote is not as toxic, but the alkaloids in this cactus are extremely bitter and their effects are long lasting. Mushrooms and peyote are eaten or soaked in hot water to make tea.

Methylenedioxymethamphetamine (MDMA) is better known as Ecstasy. This psychedelic was first manufactured

To the Spirit World

In Peru, native people collect the bark of a thick vine to make a drink called ayahuasca. This plant contains a drug called DMT (dimethyltryptamine), which is similar to LSD but even stronger. Peruvian shamans have traditionally used the drink in ceremonies. Users seem to go into a trance. They often experience dark and frightening dreamlike hallucinations. Some people become violent, as if fighting unseen enemies. The drink causes other uncomfortable side effects, including vomiting and diarrhea.

The mystery of this drug tempts some people. Travelers sometimes visit Peru just to take ayahuasca. In 2012, an 18-year-old American ventured into the jungle to visit a Peruvian shaman. His family contacted the police a few days later. The story was tragic. The young man had drunk too much ayahuasca and died. Afraid of being punished, the shaman and his helpers had buried the man in the forest. The drink had lived up to its name. Ayahuasca means "vine of death."

about a century ago. Like many synthetic hallucinogens, it was discovered by chemists seeking new medicines to solve health problems. MDMA didn't show much promise, so it was put aside for more than 50 years. It was rediscovered in the 1960s. Ecstasy became a favorite drug in the discos that opened in the late '70s. It gained even more popularity when people began to hold **raves**. At these dance parties, Ecstasy provided the energy to dance all night. The drug made people feel loving and safe, even on a crowded dance floor. It also caused some to become suddenly and dangerously ill.

Dissociatives are another category of hallucinogenic drugs. Dissociate means "to separate from." When using these drugs, people may feel as if mind and body are not connected. They often go into a trance and are unable to move. There is a good reason for that response. Ketamine and phencyclidine (PCP) are **anesthetics**, or meant to numb the nerves so no pain is felt during surgery. Both drugs are used in veterinary hospitals to treat animals. Children are sometimes given ketamine, as well. When PCP was tested on humans, patients experienced dangerous side effects. It was never approved for medical use. Sold as a cough syrup, Dextromethorphan is a substance found

Jimsonweed *(above left)*, mandrake *(below left)*, and henbane *(right)* are plants in the nightshade family, all of which cause users to lose touch with reality and may be deadly.

in many cough medicines. Although common, it can have powerful dissociative effects at certain doses.

All of the nightshades are considered **deliriants**. Jimsonweed, mandrake, and henbane are among the nightshade plants sometimes harvested from the wild to be eaten or smoked by users seeking a psychedelic "trip." Deliriants make people confused and clumsy. They lose touch with reality. The biggest problem is that deliriant users believe their hallucinations are real. When taking jimsonweed and other nightshades, people have no control over their responses. After the drug wears off, there is no memory of anything that happened. Nightshades produce several powerful alkaloids, and they can be deadly.

HALLUCINOGENIC DRUGS BY CATEGORY

	TYPE OF HALLUCINOGEN	HOW IT'S USED	STREET NAMES
PSYCHEDELICS	LSD	· swallowed · absorbed into the skin of the mouth	acid blotter microdot California sunshine
	Psilocybin mushrooms, fly agaric mushrooms	· swallowed	magic mushrooms shrooms
	Peyote cactus/ Mescaline	· swallowed · smoked	buttons mesc
	MDMA	· swallowed · snorted · injected	Ecstasy Adam peace
DISSOCIATIVES	PCP	· swallowed · snorted · injected	angel dust love boat
	Ketamine	· smoked · snorted · injected	special K
	Dextromethorphan	· swallowed	DXM, robo triple C
DELIRIANTS	Datura	· swallowed · smoked	Jimsonweed thorn apple

CHAPTER TWO

Powerful Potions

IN 1933, ARCHAEOLOGISTS FOUND A collection of Native American **artifacts** in a remote Texas cave. Among the ancient baskets and bones were a few dried objects that looked like buttons. This was not the kind of button that might have been found on clothing. They were made from ground-up plants, including small amounts of a local cactus—peyote. Chemical tests showed that the buttons were more than 5,700 years old.

This artifact is one of many proving that native people around the world used hallucinogenic plants. Tribes

Peyote cactus *(left)* and fly agaric mushrooms *(right)* are powerfully hallucinogenic plants.

in Mexico and South America worshiped peyote and psilocybin mushrooms. These plants do not grow in Siberia and other northern locales. Native people in those regions discovered the fly agaric mushroom, which is also hallucinogenic. In East India, this mushroom was known as "soma."

These substances were never taken for entertainment. People understood that hallucinogenic plants could be deadly. The drugs were carefully guarded. They were used only in special circumstances by shamans, spiritual leaders who had gone through years of training. Hallucinogens were believed to provide a connection with the spirit world. A shaman was trusted to make important decisions for the tribe. He or she used hallucinogens to ask for help when a person was sick or the community needed to solve a problem.

Hofmann's Dangerous Discovery

LSD was the first synthetic hallucinogen. In 1938, a young Swiss scientist named Albert Hofmann began to study ergot for a Swiss pharmaceutical company. He identified an alkaloid within the fungus and called it lysergic acid—LSD for short. The chemical seemed to have no obvious medical uses and was therefore shelved.

Swiss chemist Albert Hofmann accidentally discovered the hallucinogenic effects of LSD in 1943.

A few years later, Hofmann took LSD down for another test. He didn't notice when a small amount of the mixture splashed onto his hands. Within an hour, the world began to change all around him. Colors became almost painfully bright. Walls stretched and waved. Hofmann felt nauseated and dizzy. "Everything in the room spun around," he later wrote, "and the familiar objects and pieces of furniture assumed grotesque, threatening forms." Hofmann was "tripping" on LSD.

18

Despite its scary side effects, Hofmann noticed that LSD made him feel happy and free. Tests showed that LSD broke down people's fears and helped them remember things they had long forgotten. He hoped LSD might be useful in therapy, helping patients open up and talk more freely about their problems. The United States Central Intelligence Agency (CIA) had a different idea. Could LSD be used as a "truth serum" against enemy agents, forcing them to reveal their countries' secrets?

LSD was tested on animals and people in the 1950s. People were intrigued by the drug's unusual effects on color, sound, and light. Some said they felt more spiritual when using LSD. But the drug also caused rapid changes in mood, from bliss to deep sadness in seconds. Some users experienced terrible panic attacks, fearing that they would never feel normal again. Their heart rates and blood pressures skyrocketed. Nausea and vomiting left some users curled up on the floor. Hofmann and other scientists could find no way to control these reactions. For a drug to be safe in medicine, it must be reliable. Clearly LSD would not measure up to this standard.

Hofmann's pharmaceutical company decided to stop making LSD. It dropped its patent in 1963. Now anyone could manufacture and sell LSD, including "underground" labs set up in basements and warehouses. Some of these illegal labs found a way to save money. They mixed cheaper chemicals in with the LSD. As use increased during the mid-1960s, more people were treated in hospitals for "bad trips" caused by these impure drugs. In the meantime,

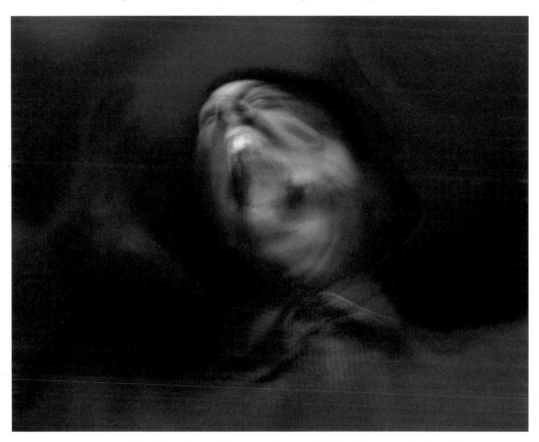

A "bad trip" on LSD can make you feel as if you are living a horror movie.

other hallucinogenic drugs such as ketamine and PCP became available. They were sold on the street and used in dance clubs. In just a short time, hallucinogens became part of popular culture.

Why Use?

In 1980, approximately 10 percent of college and high school students said they had used LSD. Within a decade, middle school students had also discovered this drug. Why do you think teens and other people take hallucinogens? When asked this question, kids list many reasons. Some of the most common include:

- to fit into a social group
- to feel more comfortable among friends and peers
- to relieve stress from pressures at school or at home
- as a way to self-medicate (relieve mental or physical pain, instead of seeing a doctor)
- curiosity—to find out what a new experience is like
- boredom—because they feel they have nothing better to do

LSD and other hallucinogens became popular with young musicians in the late 1960s. Jimi Hendrix and the Grateful Dead performed while using the drugs. Even The Beatles wrote songs about tripping on LSD. Roger "Syd" Barrett of the British band Pink Floyd dove deeply into LSD use. In 1967, Barrett suffered a mental

BREAKDOWN

breakdown just as Pink Floyd's first album became a hit. The band went on to make music history, and Barrett moved back into his mother's house in Cambridge. There he spent his time gardening, cooking, and painting. He died in 2006 at the age of 60.

Four years later, a student riot broke out on the streets of London. The British government had announced they would charge more for college tuition but spend less of that money on programs. Among the protestors was 21-year-old Charlie Gilmour. His father had taken Syd Barrett's place as guitarist for Pink Floyd in the 1960s. During the protest, Gilmour smashed a store window and threw a trash can into a line of passing cars. Police soon arrested the young man. Gilmour admitted he had taken LSD before the protest. He mixed the hallucinogen with alcohol and Valium, a strong drug that usually calms people but can have the reverse effect of causing rage. Gilmour apologized for his actions before being sent to serve several months in prison.

Young people have many reasons for experimenting with hallucinogenic drugs—and each person has a different reaction to those drugs.

- as an intentional way of rebelling or pushing the rules laid down by parents
- because they hear about them in the media and on social networking sites

The media can play a big role in drug use. Television, movies, and social media may make hallucinogens seem funny, cool, or just plain harmless. If young people don't understand that a drug is risky, they are more likely to use it. In the 1990s, kids heard a lot of anti-drug messages. They were warned about the dangers of LSD and hallucinogens. In 1993, 42 percent of eighth graders said they believed there was a great risk in trying LSD once or twice. Since that time, drug awareness programs have focused on preventing abuse of other drugs. When teens were surveyed about their drug use in 2011, less than 22 percent of eighth graders thought LSD was risky. Flip that statistic and it sends a frightening message: four out of five teens think hallucinogens are safe.

Ranking the Risk

The United States has a system for determining which drugs are most risky. In 1970, the federal government passed the Controlled Substances Act. Under this law, the Drug Enforcement Agency (DEA) evaluates drugs to compare their risks and benefits. Each drug is categorized into one of five **drug schedules**, or categories.

LSD and the other psychedelic drugs have been placed on Schedule I along with heroin and other **recreational drugs**. Substances in this category have no proven use

The federal government lists "magic" mushrooms, LSD, and other psychedelics alongside heroin as some of the most dangerous drugs available.

in medicine. Instead, they are used for personal enjoyment. Many Schedule I drugs are addictive or can cause serious health problems. By placing psychedelic drugs on Schedule I, the DEA made their use illegal. It is a felony merely to be caught with LSD in your possession. Those who sell, buy, or manufacture this drug face heavier penalties including large fines and long prison sentences.

Medicinal drugs are used to treat or prevent disease. Yet some are still abused like recreational drugs. Schedule II is a list of medicines with the greatest risk of abuse. PCP is on this list along with OxyContin, Ritalin, and methamphetamine. Health care professionals must prescribe these drugs carefully and track their use. Ketamine is a Schedule III drug. Schedules III, IV, and V contain drugs with lesser risk factors (though they are still closely monitored). It is a felony to use or possess a drug on any of these schedules without a legal doctor's prescription written especially for you.

If you doubt the risks, keep this in mind. Like all drugs, hallucinogens create their effects by changing the way your brain works. Those changes can be intense as they take place—and they can come back to haunt you for years afterward.

CHAPTER THREE

High and Low

WHAT HAPPENS WHEN YOU CONSUME LSD and other hallucinogenic drugs? At first, your body treats the drug like a typical food or beverage. After passing through your digestive system, the chemical is absorbed through the walls of the intestines into capillaries. These tiny blood vessels are connected to your circulatory system, which distributes blood throughout the body. One of the most important jobs of the circulatory system is to deliver oxygen. This molecule is the "fuel" for hardworking

Microscopic, finger-like villi line the walls of the small intestine. Each connects to the body's blood supply, moving nutrients—or drugs—throughout the body.

cells. The brain requires a lot of oxygen, so it has good blood flow. Most hallucinogens reach the brain within an hour.

Your reaction to a hallucinogen may be much stronger than that of a friend who takes the same dose. Those differences can be caused by weight and genetics. Physical responses are also influenced by other drugs that may be in your system and affected by the amount of food you've eaten recently.

Experts warn that two other factors can play especially important roles in a user's experience with hallucinogens. Those factors are set and setting. Setting refers to the environment in which a drug is used. A person who feels unsafe is at greater risk of a bad "trip." Set is an abbreviation for mindset. That includes the user's mood when taking the drug along with their expectations of how the drug will work. Anxiety, anger, and even anticipation are strong feelings. The drug produces visions and sensations to match them—pleasant and thrilling or nightmarish, depending on the emotion.

Sending Messages

Your brain is more complex than any computer. It contains billions of nerve cells that connect to the rest of your body through the central nervous system (CNS). This system works because nerve cells can send messages. Have you ever played the game Telephone? Several people stand in a line. The first one whispers something to the second, and the message is continued down the line. Telephone can be a funny game because people often forget parts of the story or mishear the message. By contrast, the nervous system is usually very accurate.

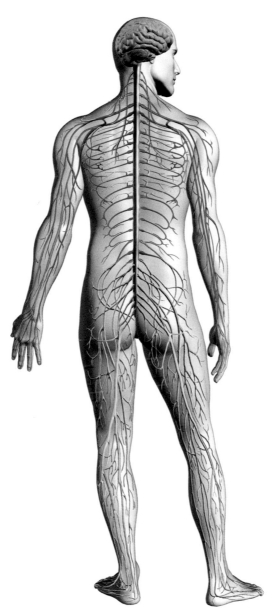

The central nervous system is a complex network of nerves that conveys signals between the brain, spinal cord, and body.

Each nerve cell is tipped with two kinds of long, finger-like branches. At one end are tufts of dendrites that bring messages into the cell. The opposite end of each nerve cell bears an arm-like axon. Reaching toward the next cell, the axon passes messages along. Signals move through nerve cells in the form of electricity. But electricity cannot flow across a **synapse**, the small, liquid space between cells. Instead, the pulse of electricity causes the axon to release chemicals called **neurotransmitters**.

Neurotransmitter molecules float across the synapse like microscopic rafts. They attach to **receptors** on nearby dendrites. Receptors can be compared to locks, while neurotransmitters are like keys. Only a matched set can fit together. When they do, an electrical signal begins to flow. In this way, messages are passed through nerve cells throughout the body. Those messages may either start or stop activity in the nervous system.

Hallucinogenic drugs cause their effects by changing the flow of certain neurotransmitter chemicals in the central nervous system. In many cases, this works because the drug happens to be shaped like a neurotransmitter. It fits into the receptor, blocking the body's chemical from doing its usual job.

Stopping Serotonin

Psychedelic drugs mimic **serotonin**. This neurotransmitter controls how intensely you react to changes in the surrounding environment. It influences many bodily processes and behaviors, from mood and alertness to digestion and body temperature. Serotonin even plays a role in visual perception, affecting how your brain interprets what you see. If you take LSD, molecules of the drug lock into the receptors that would normally hold serotonin. There is nowhere for serotonin to go, so it builds up in the synapses and blood. The same thing happens to users of mescaline, psilocybin mushrooms, and MDMA (Ecstasy).

As a psychedelic drug takes effect, the user experiences physical and emotional changes. The first sign of **intoxication** may be a feeling of pins and needles on the skin. The pupils of the eyes dilate (widen), making the person more sensitive to light. Heart rate and blood pressure increase, and the user may begin to sweat. Within a couple of hours, all the senses are affected. Sounds, smells, and colors are suddenly more intense. The user may feel a surge of emotions. The psychedelic "trip" is like a roller coaster ride. A user who feels great joy one moment can quickly shift to sorrow.

The effects of psychedelic drugs may last between six and twelve hours. In the meantime, a user may not be able to safely do even the simplest things. While walking down the street, a car's turn signal may catch their eye. To a clear-headed person, this looks like nothing more than a small, blinking light. A person on psychedelics may see it as a shimmering beacon and walk toward it without noticing the rush of traffic. Some users become **paranoid**, suspecting everyone's actions or fearing they are in danger. Others feel like superheroes. They may try to fly, or will stay outside in freezing weather without sensing the cold. These harmful side effects are called **adverse reactions**.

In 2011, two teenagers in Texas crashed their car after taking LSD. Both boys escaped alive and began to run down the street between moving cars. Neither was wearing clothes. One of the boys was thirsty, so he broke into a neighborhood house where a woman and her young son were home. The intoxicated teen told the woman he just wanted to call his mother. She sympathetically kept an eye on him until the police arrived. These teens were lucky to survive their experience. But they face a serious set of consequences. Hallucinogen use was enough

to put them in jail. Breaking and entering is a felony. Texas law allows for a prison sentence of up to 20 years in such cases.

DELIRIOUS

Dissociative drugs work by changing levels of two neurotransmitters: glutamate and dopamine. Glutamate controls our awareness of pain. It helps with learning and memory, as well as the ability to find meaning in things we sense and experience. Dopamine affects parts of the brain that control movement and emotions. It plays an important role in helping us feel both pain and enjoyment. When taking PCP or ketamine, out-of-body experiences are common. The mind and body seem completely separate. Dizziness and blurred vision may occur. The user becomes clumsy and begins to experience hallucinations. Dissociative drugs cause some people to dive into deep depression. Others stop responding to anything around them and may drool. Violent outbursts are a risk of using this dissociative, as well.

Taking too much of any dissociative drug can lead to **overdose**. The victim's body temperature soars high enough to cause brain damage, or he/she has convulsions. People sometime fall into a coma or die from the effects of these

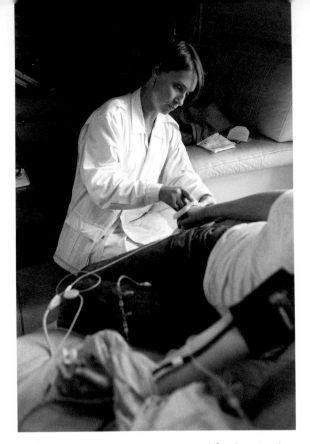

Hallucinogen overdose can cause life-threatening side effects such as high body temperature or heart attack, requiring immediate medical attention.

drugs. Drowning, falls, and other accidents also cause deaths that would have been unlikely if the person were not intoxicated. In 2006, almost 17,000 Americans wound up in emergency rooms after overdosing on Dextromethorphan. Fifty-nine percent of the patients were under the age of 21.

Several different neurotransmitters are affected by deliriant drugs. Hallucinations may begin within an hour. The person finds it hard to swallow or talk because the drug dries out their sinuses. Rapid heartbeat is a common symptom, along with blurred vision. At high doses, the nightshades can cause dangerously high body temperature or heart attack. While other hallucinogens typically clear out of the body within twelve hours, deliriants take much longer. They slow down the digestive system, making symptoms last for as much as two days.

36

BAD TRIP

Have you ever had a bad dream that seemed to go on and on? Psychedelic users may experience this feeling while they are awake. The person may begin to panic and feel as if they will never be in control again. If you are with someone who experiences a "bad trip" on hallucinogens, it is important to remain calm.

Bring your friend to a quiet room where the light is low and calming. Stay with them and keep talking in a gentle way. Remind your friend that they will feel better when the drug wears off. Stick to simple facts like your names and location. If you are patient, the symptoms should ease within a few hours.

If necessary, call a trusted adult or 911. Hallucinogens can produce reactions that require medical care. At the hospital, doctors can give drugs to ease the worst symptoms and keep panicked users from harming themselves. It's always the right choice to help a friend in need, even if you face consequences afterward.

CHAPTER FOUR

Hidden Hazards

IF YOU HAVE STREP THROAT, THE DOCTOR may prescribe an antibiotic. You'll go to a pharmacy to obtain that medication. The Food and Drug Administration (FDA) oversees the manufacturing of antibiotics and other medicinal drugs in the United States. This agency requires that medicines are pure and carefully labeled. Each pill in your antibiotic bottle will contain exactly the same dose of medicine and no other ingredients.

"Magic" mushrooms and other hallucinogens are usually grown or manufactured illegally, so users cannot be sure of their purity.

Pharmaceutical companies are careful to uphold health and safety requirements. They may lose customers or be put out of business if products don't meet FDA standards.

Most hallucinogens are made in illegal labs or collected from nature. The FDA has no control over their safety or purity. This creates serious risks. There may be no label to prove the contents and dose. No one checks to be sure that LSD and Ecstasy labs are careful when preparing their products. One dose may look just like another but contain much more of the drug. As you might guess, a larger dose increases the drug's effects and makes them last longer. The higher dose also significantly increases the risk of adverse reactions.

In 2013, a 15-year-old Australian girl almost died after taking a dose of LSD at a party. Another partygoer suffered violent hallucinations, while six teens at a local beach became so sick that they were also sent to the hospital. Police located a dealer of the blotter acid, which was decorated with an image of "Gangnam Style" singer, Psy. Tests showed that each dose was 16 times stronger than normal.

Adulteration has become another serious problem in recent years. Illegal drug labs are not concerned about your safety. These labs make drugs for profit, and they save money however possible. One of their methods is to use fillers and cheaper drugs. Ecstasy tablets collected during drug raids have been found to contain everything from talcum powder and caffeine to the highly addictive drugs amphetamine and methamphetamine.

In a single drug raid, law enforcement agents collected 100,000 Ecstasy pulls at a site in Saskatchewan, Canada.

Hooked

You have read about the intense and immediate effects that hallucinogens can have on the human body. These drugs can also cause long-term damage to users' physical and mental health.

Because the effects of hallucinogens are so long lasting, regular users often take breaks to recover. If they don't, the body may develop **tolerance** to the drug. It takes a little more of the chemical, then a little more, to create the same effects. A user who is tolerant of LSD will be tolerant of other psychedelics as well. That is because all of those drugs affect the same neurotransmitter.

Long-term use of hallucinogens can lead to **dependence**. Some drugs, including psychedelics, leave users psychologically (mentally) dependent. The user relies on a certain feeling or a state of mind produced by the drug. Dissociatives such as PCP, ketamine, and DXM can cause

QUITTING HURTS

Withdrawal is the reverse of tolerance. It is a process during which the body adjusts to not having the drug. The good news is that withdrawal passes as most of the drug leaves the body. The bad news is that it can feel like a long, terrible case of the flu with symptoms such as:

- sweating or chills
- headaches
- nausea and vomiting
- bowel problems
- restlessness
- inability to sleep
- hallucinations

physical dependence. Drugs like these change a person's body chemistry. Without them, the user feels sick and experiences **withdrawal**.

Breaking Free

The Drug Abuse Warning Network collects data on people who are hospitalized for dependence as well as drug reactions. In 2004, almost 900 Americans visited emergency

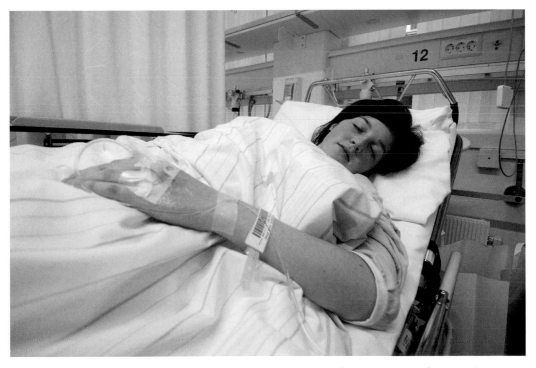

Medical treatment is sometimes necessary to ease the painful symptoms of physical dependence to dissociative drugs such as PCP, ketamine, or DXM.

rooms (ER) because of Ecstasy dependence. They needed medical help to break away from this drug. That same year more than 800 people sought help in the ER for PCP dependence. These numbers may seem small, but they are part of a worrisome trend. Within five years, hospitalizations for PCP and Ecstasy dependence had increased noticeably. In 2011, almost 4,600 Americans sought help in emergency rooms for PCP dependence. No one sets out to become addicted to drugs. But clearly, hallucinogens can have that life-changing effect.

Take the case of a 30-year-old woman who regularly used DXM. When she tried to stop, the woman experienced stomach pain, nausea, and vomiting. She was depressed, shaky, and could not sleep. After three days of miserable withdrawal symptoms, the woman visited her local emergency room. Doctors could only ease her symptoms. She finally decided to sign up for inpatient drug rehabilitation, or rehab.

Rehab is a safe place for people trying to overcome addiction. Some programs are designed especially for teens, recognizing that young people have different needs than adults. In rehab, patients have time to rest as the drugs slowly leave their system. Counselors meet with

Peer group therapy can be a source of support and comfort while learning to live without drugs.

groups and individual patients, helping them to find drug-free ways of facing challenges. Inpatient treatment isn't the right solution for everyone. Outpatient programs allow people to seek counseling and support while living at home. The individual may speak privately with a therapist, or meet with family to work through shared problems. Peer groups help teens build a support system made up of people with a similar experience. It's less expensive but requires dedication to be successful.

You might hear from peers that LSD is "safe" because it does not cause physical dependence. Don't believe it. Some people experience a condition called persistent psychosis. It's as if the side effects of LSD continue after drug itself has left the body. This problem isn't limited to long-term users. You are at risk even after a single dose. Persistent psychosis causes wild mood swings and sudden hallucinations. It can go on for years. That's what "persistent" means.

Another aftereffect of LSD use is hallucinogenic persisting perception disorder, or HPPD. You might have heard another name for these attacks: **flashbacks**. Flashbacks feel like reliving some part of a previous LSD trip. They can begin unexpectedly, months or years after the person has stopped using the drug. Lights seem to flash and objects look as if they are bent and moving. This is startling—and it can be dangerous. Imagine trying to drive, work heavy machinery, or take care of a child when such a disturbing mental change occurs. HPPD symptoms can be eased with therapy, which helps people control fear and confusion during attacks.

Other hallucinogens have lasting effects, as well. PCP users may feel depressed and experience poor memory

Months or years after stopping the use of hallucinogens, people may experience flashbacks that feel as if they have just taken the drug.

for up to a year after stopping that drug. Medical studies indicate that Ecstasy is a **neurotoxin**—it damages nerve endings. This harmful effect is especially noticeable in the brain's cerebral cortex and hippocampus. The cerebral cortex controls many essential functions of the "thinking" brain. It's in charge of memory, attention, reasoning, and planning. The hippocampus helps to store memories, so it is crucial to learning.

CHAPTER FIVE

The Big Picture

EVERY DAY, ABOUT 1,400 AMERICAN teens try LSD and other hallucinogens for the first time. Teens—and even adults—may not recognize that these drugs are risky. But there are many consequences. You have already read about a few. Hallucinogens may be impure, containing unknown drugs that can cause overdose or addiction. You can become dependent on any hallucinogen. Dissociatives even cause physical dependence that produces severe withdrawal symptoms when you try to quit. Some hallucinogens change your brain chemistry, leading to flashbacks or other mental problems after the drug use has ended.

Even if you only use hallucinogens now and then, they will impact your life. The hangover will leave you out of sorts for days afterward. You may argue more frequently with family members and feel irritated by the same friends you bonded with just days before. Meanwhile, your schoolwork will probably suffer. What about sports? It's hard to compete when you haven't eaten or slept well. Keep in mind that school sports teams can drop you for drug use. Colleges look at your school record. They may deny scholarships or even refuse acceptance if you've had a drug offense.

Don't forget that most hallucinogens are listed under the Controlled Substances Act. You can be jailed for merely having these drugs in your possession. Buying, selling, or manufacturing hallucinogens is a felony. That's a serious crime involving steep fines and years in detention or prison. A mistake like that can affect your record for years to come, blocking many future opportunities.

Reaching Out

Of course, laws can do only so much to prevent drug abuse. Perhaps the most important influence is education. Young

Your parents were once teens, too. They may understand your concerns about peer pressure or drugs and have helpful suggestions for how to solve problems and get more information.

people need to understand why hallucinogens and other recreational drugs are so risky. That begins with honest discussions between parents and kids—even if those talks are embarrassing or difficult. The DEA confirms that young people who learn a lot about the risks of drugs from their parents are up to 50 percent less likely to use drugs. With that knowledge, you become the real key to stopping

A Trip to Woodstock

The Woodstock Music Festival of 1969 brought together more than half a million young people. They gathered on a farm in Woodstock, New York, to hear a free concert by dozens of their favorite musical performers.

Woodstock was an important career break for 22-year-old Carlos Santana. His band had never played in front of a large audience. Thinking they would not perform until late in the evening, Santana and his bandmates decided to try LSD. They had heard about the drug and figured they had half a day free to experience a "trip." A couple of hours later the band received a surprising message. The schedule had changed and they were expected on stage immediately. The young musicians struggled to focus as LSD overwhelmed their senses.

Films of the concert show that Carlos Santana played with his eyes closed most of the time. Almost half a century later, Santana still recalls the sensation. "The guitar neck, it felt like an electric snake that wouldn't stand still," he told a reporter. He closed his eyes to avoid the weird image and focus on his music. As he played, Santana silently vowed to never again take LSD. His advice to others is simple: "I don't recommend it for anybody."

the cycle of drug abuse. If your parents don't bring up the subject of drugs, consider starting the conversation yourself. You can suggest searching for information on the Internet or at the library. A few resources at the back of this book will get you started.

Remember that drugs can't solve your problems—they only create new ones. Rather than escaping from reality, find caring people who will help to make your life better. If you don't feel comfortable talking with a parent, seek out an understanding family member, friend, teacher, or spiritual leader. If nothing else, find a local support group or call a hotline. It's a powerful thing to reach out and connect with others. Even one positive, caring person can make all the difference in your life. No matter how difficult things feel now, you'll be glad you didn't give away your future to drugs.

Saying No

It's not true that "everyone" does drugs. The National Survey on Drug Use and Health gathers data on drug use in America. In 2011, less than 1 percent of teens reported using LSD and only 2.4 percent said they had tried Ecstasy. The problem is that young people may not

Many young people report that they tried drugs for the first time because they felt pressure from peers or friends.

understand the risks when facing the choice of whether to try a hallucinogen. More than that, teens may not know how to refuse.

Have you ever been asked by classmates to participate in activities that break the rules or seem risky? Or felt a subtle expectation to look, dress, or behave differently to fit in? That's **peer pressure**. Many kids say that their first drug use was the result of peer pressure. It's hard to say no when you want to make friends—or when you fear being bullied for refusing. It can be hard to say no when others tell you "everyone else is doing it." Peers can be good role models, providing friendship, support, and new experiences. But they may also press you to fit in—changing the way you look or behave so you'll be more like the crowd.

When others encourage you to try something dangerous, it's time to consider their motives. People who say they have used drugs without problems may be telling the truth. Then again, adolescents sometimes make up stories about drug use or leave out their bad experiences in order to seem cool. It's also possible they are looking for someone else to take a risk they are afraid to try alone. When it comes to drugs, it's better to make your own choices. Why go along when it could harm your health?

54

Hallucinogens are social drugs. They are most commonly used at parties, after-school hangouts, and raves. So what do you do when someone invites you to try one of these drugs (or any other kind)? The DEA recommends that you give a firm but friendly response. Sometimes all you have to say is: "No, I'm not into that." Partiers will find it hard to argue when you remind them about team or school rules against using drugs. If you feel it's important to point out why drugs aren't cool, try this statement: "No thanks, I don't like how it makes people not act like themselves." Your confidence might set an example for others. And it sends a strong message if you leave when people begin using drugs. That shows you don't support their choice. It also keeps you out of trouble if adults or police arrive.

Another way to stay drug-free is by learning to manage stress. This feeling of excited nervousness may be helpful when it is mild, by keeping you focused on a new challenge. But too much stress can be exhausting. It can lead people to make unhealthy choices such as using drugs.

Here are some common signs of stress:
- Low energy, short attention span, or changes in your sleep patterns

- Anger, frustration, or crying easily
- Declining grades
- Headaches or stomachaches
- Thinking or saying bad things about yourself

If you've felt any of these, it's time to seek a healthy form of stress relief. Learn a form of meditation. This can be practiced almost anywhere, and it takes only a few minutes to quiet your mind. Sports and the arts are other outlets that focus your energy in positive directions when life seems overwhelming. Most important, learn to express your feelings. Talking with friends, parents, and other trusted adults might help your worries seem less intense.

There are many drug-free ways to enjoy your life. Get involved in groups with people who share your healthy and creative interests. Don't forget to stay active and fit. Volunteer to help others in need, or get a job to save money for college. By choosing to avoid hallucinogens, you can experience the whole journey of life—not just a trip.

GLOSSARY

adulteration to make something less pure by adding other substances to it

adverse reaction any harmful side effect of a drug

alkaloids plant-based chemicals that cause particular physical or mental reactions in animals

anesthetic a drug that kills pain, often used during surgeries

artifacts objects made by people, which have historical or cultural value

deliriants a category of hallucinogenic drugs that make people confused and clumsy in addition to producing hallucinations

dependence having an emotional or physical need for a drug

dissociatives a category of hallucinogenic drugs that makes users feel as if the mind and body are separated

dose a measured amount of a drug or medication

drug a substance that changes how the body or brain functions

drug schedule the categories used to classify drugs, based on their potential for abuse and harm

flashback a strong memory that returns repeatedly

hallucination a sight, sound, or other sensation that is not real

hallucinogens a class of drugs that change users' perception of reality

intoxication a state in which the person feels and acts drunk

medicinal drugs those used to treat or prevent disease

neurotoxin a substance that damages nerve cells

neurotransmitter chemicals that carry signals through the nervous system

overdose a large dose of a substance that causes a dangerous reaction in the body

paranoid anxious or suspicious without clear reason

peer pressure words or actions from people of the same age group that suggest a person has to act or look the same to fit in

psychedelics a category of hallucinogenic drugs that makes objects seem dreamlike and strange

rave a party involving techno music and light shows; drug use often occurs

receptor a specific site on a nerve cell to which neurotransmitters can attach

recreational drug a chemical with no medical use, taken specifically to obtain a high

serotonin a neurotransmitter involved in the control of physical responses such as mood, alertness, and appetite

shaman a person who communicates with the spirit world to heal or advise others

synapse the microscopic space between two cells in the nervous system

synthesis production of chemicals in a laboratory

tolerance a reduction in the normal effects of a drug after regular use, requiring a larger dose to obtain the same effect

withdrawal symptoms that occur when a person who is physically dependent on a drug stops its use

Find Out More

Books

Bailey, Jacqui. *Taking Action Against Drugs*. New York: Rosen Central, 2010.

LeVert, Suzanne with Jeff Hendricks. *The Facts About LSD and Other Hallucinogens.* New York: Marshall Cavendish Benchmark, 2006.

Medina, Sarah. *Know the Facts About Drugs*. New York: Rosen Central, 2010.

Rodger, Marguerite. *Party and Club Drugs.* New York: Crabtree Publishing Company, 2012.

Websites

Above the Influence

http://www.abovetheinfluence.com/

Since 1998, the National Youth Anti-Drug Media Campaign has worked in American communities empowering young people to resist the influence of drugs.

Just Think Twice

http://www.justthinktwice.com/

Prepared especially for kids by the Drug Enforcement

Agency, this site provides information about a variety of drugs commonly abused by teens and offers links for those seeking support or treatment.

Nar-Anon and Nar-Ateen

http://www.nar-anon.org

These organizations offer support for the family and friends of people addicted to drugs. Nar-Ateen meetings are especially for young people aged twelve to twenty.

Neuroscience for Kids

http://faculty.washington.edu/chudler/neurok.html

Dr. Eric H. Chudler is a biologist at the University of Washington. His website is designed to help kids better understand the nervous system.

Drug Facts: Hallucinogens

http://www.drugabuse.gov/publications/drugfacts/
hallucinogens-lsd-peyote-psilocybin-pcp

This website from the National Institute on Drug Abuse provides information on LSD, mushrooms, mescaline, and PCP.

Index

Pages in **boldface** are illustrations

CHRISTINE PETERSEN has written more than fifty books for young people, covering a wide range of topics in science, health, and social studies. In her free time, Petersen enjoys hiking and snowshoeing with her son near their home in Minneapolis, Minnesota.